Dere Mr. President

THE HILARIOUS LETTERS
KIDS WRITE TO THE PRESIDENT

Foreword by RICHARD NIXON
Introduction by ART LINKLETTER
Edited by HANNIBAL COONS
Illustrated by JOHN DeMARCO

Key Publishers, Inc.
Wheaton, Illinois

Dere Mr. President

Many years ago I came across a statement I have never forgotten. "Children make us philosophers."

That statement seems to me to capture the importance and the delight of the letters children write to the President. It reminds us that the things children say, in their own kind of wisdom, help us to re-examine the world.

I have benefited from the unique insight of the letters children write to me. There is sense and comedy, sadness and fantasy, delight and profundity in what they have to say.

It is my hope that those who read the sometimes blunt, often hilarious, but always captivating letters to "Dere Mr. President" will also be fortunate enough to share my experience when I first read them: to look at the world anew through the eyes of the young and to know that hope and faith and trust abound in the hearts of those who are young -- and in the hearts of those who have the benefits of youth's advice.

You have my thanks for bringing the wisdom of children to public attention and my best wishes always.

Richard Nixon

Contents

Introduction

When President Nixon gave me the opportunity to preserve in a book these howlingly funny letters that kids have written to him, I was naturally delighted, because I know an awful lot about kids. As M.C. of the "House Party," I talked to four of them a day for more years than I dare to remember. After all that experience, without even looking in the President's mailbag, I knew that the really great letters would be the ones from the small fry—dignified as exploding firecrackers—out of whose mouths come the hilarious, unforgettable things that no "writer" could think up in a month of Sundays.

So in the choosing of the letters for this book, I've held out for as many as possible from the little squirmers and elbow-scratchers, letters without guidance from mother or father, from teacher or principal, just earnest little kids licking a stub of a pencil and writing a letter to their President.

This way you get them untainted by adult inhibitions. Also, you catch them before anybody's taught 'em to lie. Truth isn't hard to find, it's just that adults keep trying to find something better. Little kids tell it like it is. Boy—do they! They write to the President of the United States as though he were the man at the corner gas station who helps them with their tricycle repairs. A five- or six-year-old has only a sketchy idea of what a

"President" is. He knows he's somebody pretty powerful, so he wants to get some important things said to him. He gets it said, all right. Little girls get it said too—sometimes even better.

All you have to do to uncover a mother lode of great humor is to wind up a bunch of little kids and get out of the way. That's the recipe I used for my first book, *Kids Say the Darndest Things*, and so far that one's sold four and a half million. All due to no genius of mine—it's just that you can't beat a bunch of unfettered little kids.

This book has been done the same way. Here is a look at the President's hilarious mail from kids exactly as it comes in. President Nixon laid down no conditions whatever as to which letters to include. He was content to let the kids speak for themselves, and let the blows fall where they might.

Thus, there was no eagle-eyed "selection board." There was no "screening" to choose letters that might in some way be politically advantageous. (You'll learn the truth of this quickly enough!) There was no thought given to "image," or whether the kids' folks were Republicans or Democrats. Little kids don't know a Republican *from* a Democrat—they can't spell either one! Out of their newly open kitten eyes they take a look at this world they've landed in, and usually they see it startlingly clear.

Children take a very practical view of politics, as they do of most other things. They haven't time for dogma or isms; they're too busy trying to survive. Of all the wonderful letters in this book, this one possibly best exemplifies the practical political views of kids: "Dear Mr. Nixon—I bet my friend, Gilbert, a dollar that you would win and Gilbert bet that Humphrey would win. Please win because I only have 40 cents."

Since children are unpredictable, their letters are often astonishing. They ask favors of the President that only other kids—or other parents—could believe. One little kid, as you'll see, wants the President to advance him the money for a ticket to Hollywood, so he can become a singer. Another kid says, "I'm writing to you, to try to get rid of a few cats."

Other little kids offer to do things *for* the President. They send him a nickel, or a dollar. One little girl offers to send him some cologne so he'll smell nice at his big dinners and important meetings.

A high school boy tells the President: "I have a solution to a couple of the major problems in the United States today. If you're interested, let me know." He isn't going to spend any time saving the country till he knows he has an audience!

There are letters cheering up the President, other letters that are quite harsh with him . . . kids send him teeth they've just pulled . . .

And the wonderful letters "writing back," when the kid letter writer has got an answer from *somebody* in the government—the President or a staff assistant or the head of the Treasury—and thinks he's found a pen pal. They rush to find more paper and more stamps . . . I liked the "writing back" letter that said: "Dear Mr. Presedent—Thanks a lot for the booklet. All the kids at school wanted your address."

Answer one of them, and you get hit in the head with thirty more mail sacks! That's the hazard of dealing with kids—there are so many of them. And nearly all of them can write, and if they can't write they can print . . . and they can all manage to get somebody to hoist them up so they can get the letter into the mailbox.

Most of it, fortunately, being some of the funniest stuff you've ever read.

ART LINKLETTER

Dere Mr. President

1

"What I Need, Mr. President"

Depending on age and spelling ability, kids address the President in every conceivable way. "Dere Prezedent Nixon" may turn into "Dere Mr. Noxin." Or "Dere Pres" . . . or, in a gush of punctilious formality, "Dear Mr. President Mr. Richard M. Nixon Dear Sir." Some of the children, for some unexplainable reason, address their letters to "President Milhous Nixon," and spell the Milhous correctly. Another small correspondent just started off, "Dear Nixon how are you?"

Once they decide on some form of salutation, the things kids ask the President for is beyond belief. They seemingly think of him as some sort of Big Daddy in the Sky, who can do all things possible or impossible, including everything that their parents can't or won't do:

Mr. President,

My sister has a job at a drugstore. She says that a monkey or cat is not a dependent. If it depends on you for food and water it is dependent on you; So why can't she get a refund on her income tax?

*   *   *

"I bet my friend, Gilbert, a dollar that you would win and Gilbert bet that Humphrey would win. Please win because I only have 40 cents."

I am writing to ask one favor. I can act real good, and I can ride a horse real good. Well, to get to the point I want to know if you would let me act on a TV show. The name of the show is "Rawhide." Please!

* * *

Dear Mr. Nixon,

I hope your happy we voted for you. I was lonly so I rote to you. I also wanted to ask you a question. Can I be a spy? I am 8 years old, 92 lb. And I am very good at tiptoeing.

* * *

Presidents soon learn that no matter what you do, it's very hard to please everybody:

Dear Mr. President,

You made the age to vote 18, why not make it for 8 year olds. I am 8 years old.

* * *

Will you please cancel the next astronaut launch? I will not be home that week, and were I am going there is no T.V.

* * *

Dear President Nixon,

I like you. I saw you on TV. What do you do?

* * *

May 26

Dear Richard,
I meen Mr. Nixon.
Will you please!
try to stop pallution
I am so exited
I have never
in my life wrote
a letter oh! I am
eracing and oh!
I can't find my
eracer! oh well
I will have to
say by.

Love,
Julie Teel

4

I saw you when you became President but I didn't vote for you I vote for Mr. Hubret H. Humprey.

Please do your best.

* * *

At which point, let's review the ground rules. As by now should be evident, President Nixon set up no fences around the Presidential mailbag. It was a case of Here are the letters; take your pick. These are thus all actual letters from actual kids, just as they came in, with no "screening" by the President or "doctoring" in the editing. Also, the captions on the illustrations are verbatim quotes out of actual letters.

Some of the things in the letters we don't understand ourselves. What, for instance, could a child mean by—as nearly as all of us could figure it out—"Gran Dpu Hookins"? With the younger kids it's their first attempts at handwriting, and, with the ones even younger than that, their first attempts at printing, and the result is an adventurous correspondence.

We have naturally included only parts of many of the long letters, but all the letters or portions of letters herein are just as the kids wrote them. We have added no jokes; we have altered no meanings. These are the letters that kids have written to the President. Period.

For instance:

Dear Presedent for your love and care here is a song.
God bless Amackara land that I love.
Stand beside her and gied her though the light of the might op abubv.
Through the-moutins.—Though the prars.
Through the ochens—white with foams.
God bless Amark my home sweat home.

5

Some of the kids can spell like a whiz. Most can't. Some of them, oddly, will spell the difficult words correctly and misspell the easy ones. Maybe they've looked up the hard ones. Or maybe it's just because they're kids.

Most of the children, for some reason, had a terrible time spelling "Hubert Humphrey." Nixon is a simple name to spell, but as you'll see they spelled it in all sorts of ways. Yet of many, many hundreds of letters from children of all ages and types, not one spelled "Eisenhower" wrong.

The only thing you can say for sure about a little kid is don't bet on it.

*　　*　　*

To Dere Mr. Nixion

I am 11 years old. My church youth group and I are praying for you. P.S. I need a dollar. P.S. I'll pay you bak.

*　　*　　*

Dear President Nixon

What does a President look like? I know he is a man. Is there anything special about the way he looks?

I am 6 years old and never in my whole life have I seen a President. I sure would like to see one.

If you ever come to Springfield stop by my house.

*　　*　　*

Dear President Nixon:

I'm 12, and I want to buy a B-B gun. My father doesn't exactly approve of it and I think if he will respect any opinion it will be yours.

For one, he thinks I'm not responsible enough. I don't exactly know what he means by it. I would have to lock it up, I have two small brothers. I even offered to let him lock it up and let me take it out when I asked him first. He says that I would brag to my friends, which I think anyone would, which is true. I wouldn't go and break a window or something like that. He said I would take it out to show someone and somebody would get hurt. I wouldn't hurt anybody with it and I told him that but he still doesn't trust me.

As I said before, my father would probably value your opinion, so please write back.

P.S. I earned the money myself.

* * *

(*This one's from a girl:*)

I am only a 13-year old, but I have started an organization. This organization has cleaned up 2 miles of debree just on a road of ours, which filled a city dump truck.

We have 79 more miles of debree to pick up. We only picked up two miles of debree because it was a cold day ond only 7 people showed up out of 45. If you would appoint me head of the whole state of Wisconsin teenage rubbish club we could have a lot more cleanliness in this whole United States.

* * *

Dear Mr. Pres.,

I've taken up a job of being a detectave. I'm only 9 years old. So the younger the detective, the less suspects the victim. Could you write to the Federal Bura of Investagatoin and have them send me a few pointers?

* * *

"I would like to know how to be a hero. Please answer with a note."

I was wondering if you could or would send me your San Clemente Summer Whitehouse phone number. Knowing that you like a rest from publicity, I wouldn't tell anyone. Being a responsible 8th grader, I think you could trust me to "keep my mouth shut" about it.

* * *

Dear, President Nixons

Is there such a tree as square trees in ohio? and do weepping willow trees weep? My Father I think is pulling my leg and my mother doen't know

Thank you again

Shannon G henke

Dear Mr. President,

I realize you are a busy man, indeed a very busy man. However, every time I write you, you always appoint someone to answer my mail. I appriciate the fact that my letters are answered but please, could you sign the next reply, even if someone else answers my letter? I sometimes wonder if you are really there.

*   *   *

Dear President Nixon:

I am a six year old boy. When I grow up I am going to be a spaceman. I am going to take a rocket to the moon and mine metal in the moon mountains. Then I will bring the metal back to earth and sell it. I will make $1,000,000. I want to ask you if I can use one of your government rockets and a moon-mobile.

*   *   *

(*A lot of the kids are naturally interested in space, and the astronauts, and the moon shots:*)

*   *   *

I am 8 years old. I heard you say on TV that all the people that were important and helped with the Apollo 11 are invited to Washington. Am I invited because I helped with my prayers? My mother said that does not mean me. But I think you did mean me too. Is my mother right or am I? P.S. Please let me know when to come. Can I bring my sister Kimmy too?

(And there's a row of X's for kisses. Many of the little girls, being little girls, do this.)

*   *   *

Dere President Nixon,

I was in Washington last week but I didn't get to meet you.

I am a rock collector. Maybe when the spacemen come back maybe if they have a whole lot of rocks maybe I could have a little tiny one.

I am nine years old I am going to be a hores trainer when I grow up.

*   *   *

(Many of the kids are "collectors." And to be a good collector you naturally have to ask people for things—including the President:)

I am writing to ask if you would send me some stamps, because I am a stamp coleceter and I am trying to phil the whole book. I want old ones from the United States and stamps from all over the world. Even Hawaii. Please, even send me new stamps. But please send me many of them.

*   *   *

I am a cub'scout. I have a pencil collection. And I would like one of your pencils. Will you please send me one with either your name or the name of your office? Thank you.

*   *   *

11

Dear Mr. Nixon

"HAPPY BIRTHDAY!"

Maybe it is a little late, but I hope you had a happy one.

I collect ties. If you would ask your wife maybe if she could pick out just one.

Not to mean I am begging for one but it would be a great historical addition to my collection of over 700 ties. (!) I also play drums. I entertain at banquets, parties and shows of all kinds. I will now close and I wish you again to have a happy birthday and best wishes for the next 4 years.

P.S. Don't forget to ask Pat for the ties.

*   *   *

Dear Mr. Nixon, and the secretary who is reading this,

Thought you could fool me, huh? I know how secretaries always read people's mail and answer: Signed, Richard M. Nixon.

My hobby is collecting president pictures straight from the White House. So far I have pictures from Kennedy and Johnson. This hobby of mine is kind of slow—every four or eight years. But when I'm around 99 years old I'll have lots of president pictures.

Will you please send me some pictures of President Nixon? Thank you!

*   *   *

Will you please send me a picture of the Capital and the White House. And also will you send me a 1969 penny as fast as you can.

*   *   *

"The next time you're on T.V. would you wish me a happy birthday?"

Victor Sampson
707 E. Williams
Wynnewood, Okla.

Dear Mr. President,
   I am a 11 years old boy
who would like to become
a singer. You might have
not even thought that you
were going to be president
when you were my age.
But I already know what
I am going to be. I
need help from you. All I
need from you is a round-
trip ticket to Hollywood.

            Sincerly yours,
            Victor Sampson

P. S.
You wouldn't want
to be cut out of your
future, would you?
Please I need your
help.

Dear President Nixon,

I am 8. I want to know what you do with all the old rockets that land in the sea? My father wants a rocket to send my mother to the moon. Good-by, Love.

* * *

Dear Mr. President Richard M. Nixon

How come I didn't get a birthday car from you? I got a birthday car from my Aunt Martha, my cousin Jack, my Uncle Pete and my friend Amy Lou. But I didn't get one from you. How come?

Also, could you please call me on the telephone some day. Nobody ever calls me. Not even a wrong number.

* * *

I wonder if you'd please do something for my mother.

You see, every morning after my two brothers wake up to go to school, they leave their room a big mess.

I would like to know if you would please declare my brothers' room a disaster area?

2

A Child's Garden of Good Wishes

Kids' letters to the President come in all sorts and sizes. Some are pages long, some are a single sentence. One letter consisted of: "I really haven't got anything to say, so I won't say it." A kid stuck a stamp on that and shot it off to the White House.

The stationery the letters are written on varies as much as the content. Some are on little-kid note paper, maybe topped by a "Peanuts" drawing by Mr. Schulz, or a picture of a Little League baseball player, or a little girl strolling down the Avenue in her new Easter dress . . . Others are written on lined schoolbook paper, some on paper that looks as though it might have been torn out of the side of a grocery bag. What matters is whether what you say comes from the heart.

With little kids, it always does.

In going over boxes of their letters, you suddenly make a heart-warming discovery. You suddenly realize that the writers of the last several letters didn't want anything. They were writing to their President just to wish him well, to bolster him to the extent that it lay in their power, to offer to add their little shoulders to the wheel.

16

"Dear Mr. Peresedent—I hope you got mi tooth that I sent you. I have a lot mor teeth. Doo not send the tooth bak. I have teeth aull over the hous."

Dear Mr. President:

My 9th birthday will be on August 27th. My Dad said I told everyone else about it I might as well tell you too.

If you'er ever in Neenah Wis., let me know and I will take you fishing on Lake Winnebagago. We've been getting some nice jumbo perch.

* * *

Dear Mr. Nixon,

Hi! I know you need some cheerfulness in that office on Pennsylvania Ave., so I took some time to write you this letter.

The late President Eisenhower said on inaugaration day, write to me in the White House, kids.

Well, I was just a tot then, but now I realize the importance of that highest office in the land, to uphold justice and to serve the people!

I'm not much of a speech maker, but I want to tell you that I'm proud of America, and proud to be an American. P.S. Keep up the good work!

* * *

Honorable Richard M. Nixon

My family and I are behind you all the way. Till are last Breth.

* * *

It should be emphasized that these letters are of course in no way political. Most of the kids don't know whether they're writing to a Republican, a Democrat, or a Whig. They're writing to somebody they've heard of as "the President." All the Presi-

dents throughout our history have received these wonderful letters of support from children—and they all appreciated them. There are days when any President of the United States can use a chuckle or a kind word.

From kids, he often gets both in the same letter:

Dear President Nixon,

I wanted to let you know I am very fond of you, I don't care how big your nose is. You can always count on me.

*   *   *

When we were voting for President I was for you all the time. I hope you get your picture on a stamp.

*   *   *

I saw in the New York Times that the boats from Russia are coming near Florida. I think that I know what they are going to do. When our Apollo 11 goes up they will just take pictures. I just thought I would tell you about it so you wouldn't worry.

*   *   *

(*Some of the good wishes are even shorter than that:*)

I am sending $1.00 to help the poor children.

*   *   *

(*Gifts of money to the President are, incidentally, returned with thanks.*)

*   *   *

781 Nisqually Dr
Sunnyvale, Calif
94087

Dear President Nixon,

Since I Know you
will still be around when
Kids about my age grow up
to vote you better try
at least to cut infalation
on candy.

PATRICK
Kapowich

P.S. If you write back
to me just call me
Pat
O.K. o.k.

Dear President Nixon,

I watched the inauguration on TV at school and I am very happy you are our new President. Will you please send me a few pictures of you and please send me about 3 or 4 pictures of your whole family.

P.S. I think both of your daughters and your wife are all very pretty and your O.K. too.

* * *

How is it going down at the White House? If there is anything I can do to help, send the answers back. I am going to put a dime in this letter because running the country costs lots of money.

* * *

(Some of the letters give the President helpful information:)

My zip code number is 19512. I saw you and Dwight D. Eisenhower in the paper yesterday. Dwight D. Eisenhower was President when you were Vice-President.

* * *

McKinley School was named for another famous Republican president, William McKinley of Ohio, who defeated William Jennings Bryan in 1896.

* * *

Dear President,

I am in the fifth grade. We have just finiched writing about the duties of a President. My arm all most fell off. You sure have a lot of duties. My techer put your picture by the flag. It looks nice.

* * *

Come to think of it, this book is a great textbook on how to write. (Not how to spell!) Kids instinctively know that the key to great literature is simplicity.

Some of the letters, on the other hand, make no sense at all. You can make a letter so short that nobody knows what you're talking about. Such as this one, in its entirety:

Dear Mr. President,

See you in a couple of weeks.

(Now that's overdoing it.)

* * *

Dear Presedent Nixon,

How are you? I'm nine years old. How does your wife like keeping a big house like that clean?

* * *

I would have had time to write you sooner but I did not think positive.

* * *

Dere Mr. President,

Why don't you stop riding in the state car, and start riding on a motorcycle?

       *   *   *

I am 10 years old, and I'm going to be 11 on May 12, 1969. I'm going to make my Confirmation on March 9, 1969, and I go to St. Patricks School. I'm Cathatic. I'd like to know what nationality you are.

       *   *   *

Dear Mr. R. Nixon

Thank you for taking care of our country. Here is a nickle for good conduct.

       *   *   *

Dear Nixon

I have Seen You On TV. I Was So Happy When Thay Elected You For Presint That I Jumped Up and Down Saying Yay Nixon Won. My Father Told Me To Stop Jumping So I Stoped.

Please Excuse Any Mistake I Am Only In The Thard Grade.

       *   *   *

Dear Mr. President,

I live in California.

Many people today say that the U.S. is falling apart and the people have created a rat race, e.t.c. Well, I wrote to tell you that all this isn't so.

"My teacher's little boy thought that to run for President meant you had to enter a running race. Whichever man got to the White House frist won the race and became President."

Every other summer my family takes a trip (by car) back to Toronto, Canada, where my Dad lived when he was a boy. And New Brunswick, Canada, where my mother lived, going across country you really see America first hand.

The first thing newspapers, magazine and news says is that 1. America is overcrowded. Except in the cities this is not true. Traveling through Kansas, Wyoming, Iowa and any other numerous states it's just miles and miles of just leval wheat, grass and brush, with little communities every now and again.

The other idea is 2. We are just a rat race society. This is hard to belief too. When we stopped in Hutchinson to get gas they didn't have the oil we needed so what did the gas-attendant do? Ran a block down the street to a different gas station and got us the right kind of oil!

I just wrote you all these illustrations to show you that the United States is O.K.

*   *   *

(*Mr. Humphrey may be interested to learn of one of the foul lies that helped defeat him among the tricycle set:*)

Dear Mr. Nixon,

I voted for you. But i voted H.H. first. But my girl freind said He would send us to School on Saturdays so i voted you. Oh i forgot I am nine years old.

*   *   *

"My father got your autograph for me which I keep in my own safe, under fifty books, in a bag, in a plastic bag, under a wallet, and in a secret compartment of another wallet."

This morning us 4th graders whatched you in the inauguration, And you was just fantanstic. We got to watch your inaguration and didn't have to do math.

I thought I'd let your know that my mother & father and grandmother voted for you, I don't know if my aunts and uncles voted for you or not, well the good point is that you won, that's right, isn't it. Please, President Nixon, our whole class wants a answer from you. I'm sure everyone will aburgate (?) your answer. You the lukest man that ever lived.

*   *   *

Dear President Nixon,

I saw you on t.v. your wife is very pretty. So are your daughters. Our school room got to watch you sworen in.
P.S. I'm going to do what you said. I'm going to talk softly so people will listen to my words especially my brother.

*   *   *

I am 11 years old. I have a brother named Mike. He's 10. We were both for you and we are very glad you won. Please send us some pictures of you and your family.

Last year Mike's room had an election. He represented you. But he didn't win. I'm glad you're a better speaker than he is! In our room you lost, too.
P.S. Good luck!

3

"If It Isn't Any Trouble, Could I Come and Visit You?"

You wouldn't believe how many kids ask to visit the President in the White House. Thousands of them. They write in all seriousness to ask what day they should arrive. They usually give the President a choice of arrival dates, since, as they say, they don't want to be any trouble.

Mr. Nixon,

I am 16 years old and very interested in government.

I would like to be able, if it is no trouble, to come to stay at the White House for a few days to know how it is to be a president of our fine nation. I wish this because I wish to become president someday.

Please write me the outcome as soon as possible.

Give my regards to the family.

*   *   *

I would like to No if I could visit you at the White House on the week of August 18 when I am on vacation.

*   *   *

Dear Richard M. Nixon,
May I come to
the white houses
for my birthday.

Love Suzy
Foster

Rye Ridge Rd,
Harrison, N.Y.
10528

*   *   *

Dear President Nixon,

I am seven. My father is the judge. I have been practicing my manners and would like to eat at the White House.

*   *   *

Please invite me to the White House. I will get to wear my good white dress. I am 10 years old.

* * *

Mr. Richard Nixon
President of the U.S.A.
1600 Penn. Ave.
N.W., Washington, D.C.
Dear President Nixon:

Does it cost anything to take a tour through the White House? If it does will you please tell me how much? I am in the 4th Grade. This is the last of my letter so "good-bye!"

* * *

How are things going? I wish that I could visit you in the White House, but I can't. I have two sisters and two brothers. My youngest brother is one and my oldest brother is seven. My youngest sister is a pest, but my oldest sister isn't so bad.

* * *

Mr. President,

I am a junior at Oak Glen High. I am doing my independent Research on you and what you are doing and will do for the United States of America. My parents and I will be in Washington D.C. this fall and I would like to see and speak with you if you have the time. I know I am asking a lot but it would be a great honor to me and I would be most thrilled.

I am doing this to bring up my grades. I want to attend nurses training after I graduate from High School and have to have an A-B average.

(One thing about kids—they're usually honest.)

*　　*　　*

(Sometimes they want to "visit" in a way that doesn't involve the White House at all:)

Dear Mr. Nixon this summer I feel like going up to Mount Rushmore and make a picture of you. But I am only eight years old. Maybe when I get a little bigger.

*　　*　　*

Dear President Nixon,

I am writing this letter to ask a question. This may sound silly and it's kind of a lot to ask, but would it be all right for me to go inside Air Force I? Because: 1) I love airplanes; 2) I'd like to be an airline pilot or the president's pilot when I am older; and 3) I have never been inside a 707.

I went to Orange County Airport (near the President's West Coast White House) the day you landed there because I wanted to see you and Air Force 1. When I got back I decided to write a story about what I saw and heard, which by the way was all very exciting. If you happen to see Lt. Colonel Albertazzie please tell him for me, he made a very good landing and a very good take-off.

I'm putting the story that I was telling you about in this letter. I hope you like it.

Hope you enjoy your stay in Orange County.

* * *

(*Following is a small boy's report of the President's arrival at the Summer White House:*)

"There she is!," as a 707 came looming up. "Yep, that's it!" "Boy, she's gonna be low over the San Diego Freeway!"

The date is August 9, 1969, 8,000 people are gathered at Orange County Airport and are waiting very excitedly for President Nixon and Air Force 1!

Everyone is tense. Lt. Colonel Ralph Albertazzie, the pilot of Air Force 1, is bringing the huge bird in very slowly and carefully. The fire trucks are ready in case of an emergency. Everybody is hoping they don't have to use those firetrucks! The big bird is within hearing distance now. The nose is high. Touchdown! President Nixon and Air Force 1 are down! The crowds are cheering! "Hurrah, for President Nixon! Hurray"

The plane has stopped and is turning to get off the runway. Although most of the crowd thought that the 707 would have to use the whole runway Lt. Colonel Albertazzie has stopped the big bird in half the runway. He didn't even use the amount of reverse thrust he normally uses! This is because most of their fuel has been used up and the plane is much lighter than when they took off.

The plane has taxied from the runway and is stopping at Gate 3. The door flies open and out steps President Nixon! The crowd cheers! The band plays! President Nixon and his wife Pat walk

32

down the passenger ramp and step onto solid ground. Almost instantly they are surrounded by hundreds of people, it seems.

The president makes a short speech and then shakes hands with some people. He then walks to Army 1 the president's helicopter.

The helicopter taxis out to the runway and takes off. President Nixon is on his way to San Clemente.

A few minutes later Air Force 1 takes off and goes to El Toro Marine Base.

It has been a very exciting event for Orange County.

(And where could you read a better report of a Presidential plane arrival than that?)

*　　*　　*

In addition to all the kids who would like to visit the President at the White House "if it isn't any trouble," another batch are inviting the President to visit them:

Dear Mr. President,

I saw your daughter's picture in the paper cutting the cake and would like to wish her a happy birthday. My brother's birthday was on Thursday. Would you like to come and rest at our house comming back from Europe before you go back to the White House? We have four bedrooms. We promise not to tell anybody that you are comming so you can have a peaceful night. I am ten years old. We have a fireplace and I heard that you like fires.

*　　*　　*

"Dear Mr. Nixon, I have 6 sister and 1 brother add it up and
it's 7 but add me up to and it's 8. Our house is petty crowded
we have a dog to and are parents and we only have a little
house but we all fit in it."

I am asking if you can come over some time. I voted for you eaven tho I am a kid.

Well, I will tell you my address it is Pipersville, Pa. We live in a house that is white and green on the botem and a gray mail box.

I hope you can come.

*   *   *

Thank you for the pin and the handsome picture. Will you come to see us.

I love you.

*   *   *

(*Oddly, many of the most hospitable letters come from homes that already seem a little crowded:*)

Some day will you sleep over, I aske my dad and he said it would be alright. You are going to sleep in a double bed, my brother's are going to sleep in a bunk, Mom, Dad, will sleep in the other double bed, and I will sleep on the sofa.

*   *   *

I live near Washington. You could land your helicopter in the high school field near our house (if you don't mind climbing through the hole in the fence). Drop in and I'll play you a song or two on my guitar.

*   *   *

Dear Miss Rosemary Woods (President Nixon's personal secretary),

You are invited to come to my house anytime between Dec. 24–Jan. 1. If you don't come I will be very disappointed. Please tell Richard Nixon, Spiro Agnew, Robert Finch and Melvin Laird that they are invited. I would like them to come very much. Will you please send me up 1 big box of Whitehouse stationary? I would very much like to have some.

Part of the problems of today's government is that the goverment officials and the President don't take enough time to talk and visit today's teenagers.

Think about this when you refuse my invitation.

* * *

(There are of course quite a few stacks of letters from kids inviting the President to come and visit various schools:)

Dear Mr. and Mrs. Nixon:

On our last day of school picnic which comes on May 28, at 11 o'clock our fourth grade class is having a picnic dinner and "fun-in", in the yard of one of our students. Our lunch (really it will be a dinner) will include home fried chicken, devilled eggs, home made ice cream, and all the good American trimmings. If you come, we will recite for you in choral reading the exciting patriotic verses, 34 for 34 of us, that we are preparing to present at our Awards Assembly.

We have a wonderful school and principal. We think he's really cool. Our teacher is hep, too! We hope you can come.

* * *

923 N Edgemont St
Los Angeles, Calif 90029
August 19, 1969

Dear President Nixon,
      My Mother taught
us boys not to put our elbows
on the table, didn'n yours?

      We enjoyed watching
the State dinner very much.

      Respectfully,

      James Grant age 12
      Paul Grant age 11
      John Grant age 9
      Mark Grant age 7

Dear President Nixon,

Will you please make a visit to our school. We would like to know why we have to have the subject English. We already know how to talk. Would you write to tell us the day that you could make it. Would you please talk to our principle about English, too. Could you make the visit before June 10? If you can't we won't be able to be there, because we are in sixth grade now and we will be going to a different school. English is too complicated.

*　　*　　*

(*President Nixon's announcement of the Los Angeles dinner for the astronauts brought a flood of letters from kids wanting to attend:*)

My dear Mr. President:

I heard on television that you are going to give a dinner on August 13th for the astronauts in their honor.

I am 11 years of age. I would be highly elated if you would please invite me to the dinner. My greatest wish would be to be in your presence and be able to praise Mr. Armstrong, Collins an Aldrin for their accomplishment. I would truly like to see and touch them myself.

Excuse me, but if I am invited I must have one or both of parents with me as I am too young to be alone.

*　　*　　*

I just heard about the dinner for the astronauts on the 13th of August. My birthday is also on the 13th of August, it will be my 12th birthday. The thing I would like most in the whole world is to be at the dinner and meet the astronauts.

P.S. If it is too expensive for you I would be glad to pay for my dinner.

4

"One of Your Two New Dogs Looks Like My Grandmother"

When you're dealing with children, some of the proceedings will naturally concern pets. The President's mail from kids is no exception. Many of his most heartfelt letters are about pets.

Dear Mr. Nixion,

I don't know much about you but I sure hope you will read the rest of this letter.

I live in a town between Seattle and Tacoma, in Washington. I have always wanted a horse. Ever since I was 7-1/2 I have wished for a horse. I am now 14. I made the Honor roll at school, and I love animals. You don't know how much a horse would mean to me! My parents say, "If you find a free horse, We'll let you keep him." My parents say that we don't have any place to keep it, but I know of a place. All of my friends have horses but me.

If you would buy me a horse or send me the money for one you don't know how much it would mean to me. It doesn't have to be a prize winning one. Just a freindly one.

* * *

"Do you have a pet. If you have a dog get rid of it because we have a dog and he is a nut you can't sleep you can't do anything with that dog."

Hi! How are you doing my Family has 600 chickens and 2 sick ones. And a cat. Please writ back.

*   *   *

(*Many of the pet lovers, for some reason, aren't overly gabby:*)

My brother knew you were going to win the election. So he named his cat after you.

*   *   *

I am a ten year old girl that loves animals and reading. I have two questions I would like answered. They are: What pets do you own and what are their names? Also what happens when you reach the age of one hundred?

*   *   *

I don't know what happens when you reach the age of one hundred—except that you have to put a lot of candles on your birthday cake.

As for the other above question, the Nixons have three dogs— a poodle named Vicky, a terrier named Pasha, and an Irish Setter named King Timahoe. At least that's the count as of the moment. The President's pets, like other people's pets, are subject to change.

By happenstance, the President's new Irish setter brought a spate of correspondence from the junior set. A photographer took a picture of the President taking his new Irisher for a walk around the White House lawn, and, as luck would have it, one of the dog's hindlegs was exactly shielded by his other hindleg so it looked as though the dog had only three legs. The picture was widely circulated, and there were quite a few letters to the President about it. Such as this one, on Cub Scout stationery:

Dear President Nixon,

The enclosed picture of you and your dog appeared in my "Weekly Reader" at school. Does your poor dog really only have three legs or four like a real dog?

* * *

Like all the suddenly famous, King Timahoe even received an offer of marriage:

Dear President Nixon,

We have a Irish Setter. Her name is Irish Tinker Belle. She is very Beautiful.

I would like to kno if your setter King Timahoe would like to marry our Belle.

* * *

(Many of the kids' letters will leap from one subject to another:)

Dear Sur

I think that if someone has a dog or a cat or some kind of animal they should get money back for there food and shots' in there income tax. And you will never be able to stop the draf because it is a coutry full of chickens.

* * *

"We have a dog, and when you here what his breed is you'll laugh! It's a poohcock which means Part Poodle and Cocker-spanial."

Judging from the President's letters from kids, the cats of the world can take heart. They have a lot of staunch little friends.

Dear President Nixon,

Winston Churchill had a cat. All the Prime Ministers have cats. Why don't Presidents have them? As far as I know the last president to own a cat was William Taft. It would make a good image for you.

*   *   *

The above information on the White House cats differs sharply from the country's leading expert on the subject—Margaret Truman. Margaret has just written a thoroughly delightful book, White House Pets, *which tells about all the pets who have ever lived at the White House, from George Washington's horses and hounds to Mr. Nixon's King Timahoe.*

According to Margaret, who writes as though she knows what she's talking about, William Howard Taft didn't have a cat; he had a cow, named for some reason Pauline Wayne. You wouldn't believe some of the names the Presidents have given to their pets.

But for the moment, let's stick to cats. Prior to William Taft, Abraham Lincoln had some cats. Theodore Roosevelt had two cats named Tom Quartz and Slippers, and, since Taft, Calvin Coolidge had two cats—an alley cat named Tiger and another cat named Blacky—and John F. Kennedy had a cat named Tom Kitten. And earlier, Martin Van Buren had cats, in a way; he had two tiger cubs.

Theodore Roosevelt, being the sort of outdoor man he was and having a lot of adventurous sons around the White House, naturally had the most pets . . . a collection roughly akin to

45

"If you want a free kitten you can have your pick of a white one with a spot on its forehead. Or a black one with Blue eyes. P.S. I wrote this letter to get rid of a few cats."

the average zoo . . . but who do you think ran him a close second in number of pets? You couldn't guess in a hundred years. Calvin Coolidge! Possibly the least known of all our Presidents, quiet little Mr. Coolidge had a terrier named Peter Pan, an airedale named Paul Pry, a white collie named Rob Roy, another white collie named Prudence Prim, a shetland sheepdog named Calamity Jane, two chow dogs named Tiny Tim and Blackberry, a brown collie named Ruby Rough, a bulldog named Boston Beans, a police dog named King Kole, a yellow collie named Bessie, a bird dog named Palo Alto, two canaries named Nip and Tuck, a white canary named Snowflake, a thrush named Old Bill, a goose named Enoch, a mockingbird who was the personal pet of Mrs. Coolidge, the two cats, Tiger and Blacky, a couple of raccoons named Rebecca and Horace, a donkey named Ebenezer, a bobcat named Smokey, and some lion cubs, a wallaby, a pigmy hippo, and a bear.

Kids, the next time your parents complain about those two hamsters you've got, or that nice little dog who's followed you home from school, tell them about Coolidge! They'll be so amazed that they'll let you keep the dog.

Even better, get Margaret Truman's book about all the White House pets and let them read that. They'll never complain about your pets again.

*   *   *

Dear President Nixon.

I wrote this letter to give you some advice. Sell two of your dogs and get either a kitten or a cat. And they will not fight because we have two dogs and a kitten and a bird.

And not one of them fight. I hope you will write me back.

*   *   *

"By the way, during your parade in Baltimore, did you see blonde haired girl holding a Siamese cat on the roof of a blue Buick? That was me."

I like everyone like you do Mr. Nixon. And I work as hard as I can Mr. Nixon. Our dog is white and black and and he likes anyone he sees. Our birds are yellow and Red they are very prttybirds. We have a dog and birds.

*   *   *

I think you are the best man in the world. Do you think so? Will you please send me your atcraf. And a pitcher of you and your family and dogs. I might send you a pitcher of me. Whell I have to go to bed now.
P.S. I cant send you my pitcher.

*   *   *

Sometimes I think animals and apes are smarter than us because they don't drop bom's on each other.

*   *   *

Dear President Nixon,
I voted for you.
What are you going to do for the coutry? I have a cat and fishes.

*   *   *

Today my cow had her first calf. Since it is your birthday I named her Nixie.
Both my parents are Republicanss and I plan to be one too.
I am eight years old. I would like for you to come and see Nixie and me.

*   *   *

Dear President Nixon,

I like you very much. I am very sad Eisenhower died. In my Weekly Reader it said you have two new dogs. One of them looks like my grandmother.

5

The President's
Pen Pals

The President's correspondence with children contains an unavoidable pitfall. If he answers them, they answer him, and if he answers once more, all their brothers and sisters and friends and classmates write him, and suddenly the mailbag at the White House is so heavy that the postman sprains his back. In the White House mail room, this is known as the Snowball Syndrome.

A letter from a little girl will illustrate what we mean.

Dear President-Elect Nixon:

Thank you very much for the card you sent me. I brought that card to school and everybody went crazy over it. They all asked me for your address. (!) There are many people in our class who wrote to you, mostly all girls, cause they think you are cool, in fact my girl friend says she digs you. I say that too. I have to say good-bye now, but I will write back. Bye. Luv.

* * *

"Dere Mr. Prezident—When I got your letter I just about fell over flat."

Our next saga of the mailbag started innocently enough:

Dear President Nixon:

We are in second grade. We hope you like being President. If we could vote, some of us would vote for you.

From you friends, Classroom 104.

P.S. We read about President Lincoln getting a letter from a little girl saying he would be better looking with a beard. All 24 of us took a vote, and 19 hope that you never grow a beard.

P.S. Number Two. We are sending you some picture of how we think you would look.

The letter was signed by all 24 of the children in Classroom 104.

Then the Snowball Syndrome arose. A local newspaper heard of the letter the kids had written to the President and ran it in the paper. This prompted the teacher to forward to the President the newspaper report plus the following letter:

Dear President Nixon,

Enclosed is a news article of a project completed by the children of my second grade class.

During my years of teaching, I have found that small children usually are very patriotic. They seem to have great love of their Country, their Flag and of their President. They are thrilled by stories of Famous Americans and of Great Heroes. I wonder why there seems to be so little "carry-over" in many of our youths of today.

The children followed the election very closely. We have had several bulletin boards consisting of news clippings.

This is only a suggestion on my part—Children are very

impressed and delighted with something they can *see* and *hold* and *keep*.

Do you think it would be possible to send each child a picture of your dogs? Since they can't sign their names, could they put a dog paw (finger print) on the corner of the picture? We now have 25 pupils rather than 24.

* * *

The above letter was on March 26. On May 24, there was another communiqué from the teacher. There was evidently something so genuine about her original letter that the President had sent along the dog pictures (though no further mention was made of the paw prints), and the teacher was now answering that letter, which, after all, is only the polite thing to do:

Dear President Nixon,

How delighted the children were when your letter and the photos of your dogs arrived at our classroom!

The children want to show their appreciation by sending you a tape which they enjoyed making.

You may be interested to know that our school is over one hundred years old. It is located in the oldest section of the city. Much urban renewal work is taking place. The children come from low-income homes.

Your response to their letter and drawings of March 24th has put a very meaningful conclusion to our Study Unit about the Post Office.

(Something about this letter brought forth another answer from the White House. Which, on June 2nd, brought forth this answer to that letter:)

What a grand surprise to have the large brown envelope arrive from the White House! We were all delighted.

Since this school is in a socially disadvantaged area of the city, the response to the children's letter and pictures had great meaning for the children.

Thanks for your interest and kindness.

(And there you have the Snowball Syndrome. You also have an explanation of why the President and his White House staff often go to great lengths to make a few children, or even one child, happy.)

* * *

I got your letter last Friday. I brought it to school today and everybody just fliped. Some people were so hesterical that they wanted to touch Me and the envelop. And here is the most important thing I wanted to tell you is that I want to be assistant cook or servant boy PLEASE. Because I would like to serve you your meals and dust and the school would send Me my school work. And if you want to know how smart I am I am one of the smartest kids in our class. And I would like to work with you very much. PLEASE!

P.S. If a secretary is reading this please take it right up to Mr. Nixon this letter is personal.

* * *

Dear Mr. Nixson,

You probably think I have some nerve to write to the President. Well, maybe you will answer. (I hope.)

Age 11, sixth grade, brown hair, blue eyes, and 5'! That's me. I spent a whole night planning this letter. I would like to become Pen-Pals because I can help you and you can help me with my problems. You can think about it and write. I must go to bed, so fare well.

* * *

(The wonderfully scatterbrained quality of a child's mind is nowhere better exemplified than in these letters to the President:)

How are you and your family. I thank you for answering my letter.

President Nixon you don't know what your letters mean to me, it means a great deal, like a reward. Every letter I receive from you I will put in a frame. I would have wrote sooner but I forgot about you.

* * *

(On the other hand, some of the kids answer by return mail, wanting to cement their new relationship with the President without delay:)

Dear President Nixon,

How are you? I'm all right and so's the family. Your booklet arrived today. I love it already and I'll treasure it for the rest of my life. You've made me very happy. At first I thought it was for Daddy. How is Mrs. Eisenhower? I hope she's all right. I earned thirty cents this morning dusting for the neighbor lady. She gave me this letter paper, envelope and a place mat. Oh, I do thank your staff assistant for the note telling me about the booklet. I thank him, too. Happy Easter to all!

* * *

One little kid just started off: "Dear Mr. Nixon—Boy, is it raining in Arizona."

Since little children know all about their own doings, and since they have no real knowledge about what a President does, it's only natural that they should assume that the President knows, and remembers, all about them. This can result in some fairly confusing letters when the President's staff sends something to a child, and some other child in the family writes back:

Dear Mr. Nixon,

I'm glad you came to California. I'm the twin sister to Eileen. She sent you a note before. I'm glad you sent the pitcher to Eileen you look good even if it is Eileen's pitcher.

* * *

(Some of the children have difficulty deciding where to put their capital letters:)

dear President Nixon,

I thank you for the letter you gift to me. I like you because you are the best President I see. And I like your hand writer. And I want to have a other letter like my sister does, but this is the ENd.

* * *

My brother just graduated from eighth grade. And he said you wrote them a letter saying you graduated from Roxbury High school also. Is this ture?

* * *

"I am a boy. I have three sisters and no brothers. In a republican family, I feel like a democrat with laringidias."

(Some of the letters from the little kids "writing back" are utterly incomprehensible:)

Dear Mrs. Woods

I think you know my name. The first letter I sent to President Nixon you couldn't help me. But a few months later they did our street. Thank you very much.

*   *   *

Dear Mr. President: XOXOXO Kisses for you. I have a book call We, the People. My Daddy got it. Thank you for thinking of the valentine I gave you. Did you know I love you. We didn't have good weather in California until the sun came out. Did you know I am a good citizen because I am a brownie. And every brownie is a good citizen. And my brownie promise. I promise to do my best to love God and my country, to help other people every day, especially those at home. And you are invited to my birthday party. I will be 8 years old.

*   *   *

Dear Mr. President,

I loved your book the minute I saw it. I hope you can write letters back. Here is a picture of me and my little sister. I will send you a letter soon. You will be getting more letters from my friends at school, because I showed the book to them. I do not want to keep you busy but just had to show it. I am very sorry that I did not get to write to you but I had so much to do so if you think I forgot you you are wrong because it is only because of the mail. I have decided that if you have a minute I would like you to write a little letter of your's alone. I will try to send you pictures of many other places I have lived. I just love to write letter's to you. I could spend all night. I am going to sleep now so I will write to you when I wake up so good-night. I have woke up now so I will start again. I am named after my father. There are 6 children in my family counting me. I have a pet hamster named Rusty. We have a very big house and a big fire place. I do not know how long it will take to get this to you. I think this is enough letter so I think I had better quit so good-bye and here is a poem I wrote by myself.

POEM

If I were a flag,
Flying in the sky,
Standing very high,
Seeing evrey sight,
Fighting for the right
I think I would be happy,
Standing there so bright.

*   *   *

(*Some of the letters, even the ones "writing back," are of course shorter:*)

Dear Mr. President,

I wrote you earlier regarding the Biafia/Nigeria situation. I stated that I thought we should be able to send more aid, because it seems we always have enough money for wars, AbMS, and moon projects. You replied and said you could not answer fully at that time, so I decided to write and see if you could answer fully now.

Dear President Nixon,

Thank you very much for the booklets. I am just curious if you are left or right handed. I am left, my sister is right, our whole family right except me and Uncle Walt.

*   *   *

Dear President Nixon,
I Dream about being the first space boy.
I would like to do it very much!
My Mom said that she would miss me,
But she said it will be all right.
I have a picture of me,
Will you send a picture of you?
I am going into 3rd grade.
I am going to wake up and watch
the astonauts in apollo 11.

P.S. I am 7 and I hope you
have a nice summer!
Your friend: Greg

Greg Magnuson
4640 Gertrude Dr.
Fremont calif. 94536

I enjoyed everything in the booklet and even on the envelope because I have never even seen the Einstein postage stamp.

There was one thing about it that my sister did not enjoy. Becuse when I got it I yelled so loud with happiness that she could not hear the television!

I was surprised when I read about your school subjects and activities because History is my favorite subject and this being my first year having the subject I was very interested in the Constitoution. And on top of all that football is my favorite sport.

Since this booklet tells a lot about you I will tell you something about me. I am eleven years old. My birthday is September 17. I like outdoors. My average school grades are A's and B's and occasionally a C or two. You might not be interested in this I wrote it just in case you were.

*   *   *

Next we come to a batch of "writing back" letters from the fifth grade of a school in Chicago, Illinois. It is seemingly an all-Negro school, or nearly so, and they're a swinging bunch of kids.

They first wrote to the President to ask that a national holiday be established for Martin Luther King. Okay, other school classes have done that. But these kids also wrote to their senators, and their state senators.

When one of their class called the White House to find out if the President had read their letters, he was told that the President got so many letters that he naturally had a problem trying to read them all.

So these kids wrote another barrage of thirty letters, advising the President on how to read his mail:

63

I know the President is very busy every day. He gets letters from all over the U.S. Will you please tell him to put 51 bulletin boards around his room and all the letters from Illinois, Kansas and the rest put them on the right bulletin board. When he has time to read these letters he can go around the room and read them all.

This particular bunch of Chicago kids write the President— and practically everybody else who can read—about practically anything:

President Nixon, a freind of ours is in trouble for not filing his income tax. My classmates and I feel he should be in the hospital helping his patients. I was wondering if you would help us to get him out of jail.

And these from the same kids:

We have sent the children of Biafra $61.04 . . .

We solve problems by: Finding out what the problem is, discuss the problem, make solution for the problem, pick the best solution and solve the problem . . .

We have been writing to many people. Brotherhood means friendship so we had written to different kinds of schools. We have been writing to white schools and visiting each other back and forth. We learn a lot from these trips . . .

We have been trying to go to Springfield. We went to the Ill. Bell Telephone Co. asking them if they could donate two buses for us to go to Springfield. We had a meeting with the parents of the fifth grade students of our school. Some of the parents said that they will help us.

Please help us.

Merci Beaucoup.

6

"One of My Constituents..."

Some of the kids' letters arrive at the White House with what you might call a motorcycle escort. These are the letters that are forwarded with an accompanying note from a Senator or Congressman, the principal of a large school, the local head of the Save The Redwoods Committee, or some other prominent citizen. In some of these accompanying letters from Congressmen it is possible to detect a slight amount of tongue-in-cheek.

Dear Mr. President:

Enclosed is a copy of a letter from a young constituent of mine who has a suggestion about the renaming of Pennsylvania Avenue.

(And the enclosed letter:)

I have a complaint.

I am eleven years old. This year in the fifth grade we studied about the branches of government. We also studied about the streets and places in Washington. My history book said the President lived on Pennsylvania Avenue. I know this is true because I've been there.

My complaint is this. Pennsylvania Avenue should be called something such as States Avenue, U.S.A. Avenue, or Capitol Avenue, but nothing pertaining to any certain state.

* * *

(*Or this one shepherded in by another member of Congress:*)

Enclosed is the prize essay of a young constituent of mine. She asked me to personally deliver her essay to you, expressing concern that you would never see it if it was mailed to you.

I explained to her that personal contact with the President is not always possible in view of your very heavy schedule, but I assured her that her essay would indeed be brought to your attention even if sent to you through the mail.

An acknowledgement to her over your personal signature will be deeply appreciated.

(*The essay in question says in part:*)

WHAT AMERICA MEANS TO ME

. . . This is America, the land of beauty, filled with bubbling laughter and hope of opportunity . . .

Men scan the ocean bottom and soar through blackened, empty space, all in search of something. I call to everyone, "Look to youth," America's backbone. I have the stamina, energy and bright, alert ideas awakening. My buds will make tomorrow brighter if they are watered with tenderness and mellowed with kindness and understanding today . . .

All of these things tied together by one wheat strand and stuffed in a kernel of corn, which are carted through dark coal mines and over steep mountains, are what America means to me!

* * *

This is the sort of thing that can set schoolteachers' hearts to pounding, and parents' eyes to misting. Suddenly the little child you once knew is standing up there on life's big stage straight and tall, and saying noble things. That is the world out there, and we, the young people, are going to make it a better world. And who knows—maybe they will.

* * *

Sometimes the intercession by members of Congress is not the result of an original missive to them, but a last-resort appeal from a disappointed letter writer. Many of the children's letters to the President are rerouted to whichever division of the government they seem to concern, and since the people in government are quite a bit like the people out of government, some of these letters get to somebody's desk on one of those days when everything's hitting the fan. You're up to your ears in problems, and here comes a letter from some damp-nosed child wanting to move the capitol to Toledo. The result is that children can get a brusque answer.

Such a chain of events erupted one morning in the mailbag of a Senator:

I am a school teacher. As a creative writing and design activity I asked my two sixth grade language classes to 1. think of a stamp design they would like to see made into a real stamp, 2. design the stamp on paper, and 3. write a letter telling why they thought their stamps were good suggestions. A lot of time, thought and work on their part went into them and we were all pleased with the results. I had planned on exhibiting them in the room when one child suggested that perhaps the President might like to see them! Not wanting to put a damper on their idea and enjoying their interest in the project, I gave the child permission to mail them.

Yesterday, after several weeks of ANXIOUS waiting for hopefully some small acknowledgement from the President, this letter came in the mail that I am attaching. I am sure you can realize the disappointment of sixty children if they were to read the letter and see their returned stamps! Therefore, I am hoping that you can perhaps somehow forward these to a public relations secretary of the President in the hopes that they will receive a more appreciative, thoughtful reply.

Thanks very much.

(The enclosed letter that the kids had received after slaving away on their stamp designs was as follows:)

POST OFFICE DEPARTMENT
Washington, D.C.

Dear Students:

Your recent letters and designs transmitted to the President have been referred to this office for attention.

You are to be commended for your interest in our postage stamps and the designs are most interesting. However, since there are no stamps pending for these subjects at this time, we are returning your sketches.

P.S. The Apollo stamp has already been designed.

* * *

But the Senator filled in the breach, and the kids finally got a nice letter, right from the White House.

The government does like kids. The government is made up of men and women most of whom have children and grandchildren of their own. Like parents and grandparents everywhere, they will go to a lot of trouble to make their kids, and your kids, happy.

68

Dear President Nixon,

As one of your Voter, I would like you to send children to Mars. I would appreciate it very much if I could go.

your Voter
Mitchell Miller

I live at 11 Galping Hill Rd. Holmedel N.J.

Dear President Nixon,
As the parents of Mitchell Miller, age 8, I would like to give you our permission to send him to Mars!
Mr. & Mrs. Merill Miller

(Some of the letters from the adults are pretty funny too:)

Mr. Presidential Press Secretary
Dear Sir:

Around three weeks ago the Portland "Oregonian" published a letter written by our beloved President Nixon to a little boy, in answer to his inquiring about "love" or "freedom" I do not remember exactly, entitled "Nixon Writes Boy Letter." This letter was outstanding, so much so that I cut it out of the paper for use at Vespers service for resident Camp Fire Girls July 17.

At a meeting in our Park the wind came up in my absence and blew it away. Would it be possible for you to send me a copy?

* * *

Many teachers write to the President, enclosing one to a jillion letters from their pupils. Many of these teachers are in the disadvantaged areas, and they are quite evidently using "writing to the President" as another effort to get their pupils intellectually enlivened. Which is as good a reason for using a postage stamp as any.

Incidentally, thirty feet away from a table laden with children's letters to the President, you can unerringly spot the letters from teachers. The handwriting is so beautiful. In addition to everything else children were once taught in school, whatever happened to penmanship? As one little girl said, "I know my handwriting looks like a fly fell in the inkwell and walked around on the paper." (That it does—that it does!)

But the teachers' handwriting is beautiful:

Dear President Nixon,

Enclosed is an original essay which you might enjoy reading. The author is a seven-year old. Shortly after watching your inauguration, I assigned the topic, "If I were president what would I do to help make America a better place to live?" For a second grader, I feel Susan's essay shows unusual compassion.

(*And here is Susan's essay:*)

If I were a president I would do something about the car wrecks. I will help people who could not afford clothes. And old folk who do not have good homes. I will help kids who don't go to school. I will help the people who kill and steal. I will help the people who get sick and dies. I will help the family who don't have enough of food to eat. I will help the truck wrecks. And there's lot of other things happening, to.

* * *

Sometimes a teacher, despairing of the probability of the President reading a whole batch of letters, writes what you might call an "umbrella" letter and has all the kids sign it:

Dear President Nixon,

We are children from Brooklyn.

We hope that you can help improve our country while you are our President.

We think that *all* Americans should have nice homes and be able to get a good education.

Can you please answer our letter and tell us how you are going to make America a better place to live?

Thank you for your consideration.

(*Signed by 25 little nippers—mostly printed.*)

Dear Mr. President,

You may think this request strange, but I believe you should grow side-burns. Everyone (practiclly) is wearing them, and I think you would look cool with them. Your tring to identify with us, the young people, and this might make it easier on you. You don't have to worry, my folks are Republicans.

Karen
McVeigh
7th grade
Lake Geneva,
Wisconsin

(And from clear across the country in California:)

My Dear Mr. President:

Enclosed is a letter from two of my second grade boys. They are both very superior pupils, and have done research on a number of subjects of their own choice as well as extra work on our regular units of school work.

They really composed the enclosed letter, but I did make sure the words were spelled correctly. There was a serious discussion as to whether to use manuscript writing* or their newly learned cursive, which doesn't go so fast! They each wrote parts of the letter.

The boys will be thrilled to hear from their President.

(And the boys' letter:)

Dear President Nixon:

We have been studying at school about the President's Seal. We got interested in it at the time of the election and especially at the time of the inauguration. We wondered how it came about that this Seal became the Seal of the President on a banner. We decided to look up all we could find out about the Seal.

We used our library and the Encyclopedia Brittanica. In the Encyclopedia we learned about the men who designed it and the changes that were made over the years before the design was adopted for the official Seal. But we could not find how the Seal became to be used as a Presidential banner. And we could not find why they used arrows, the branch and other symbols. We know that the 13 arrows mean the first 13 states, but weren't able to find too much about the symbols.

* (Ed. note: I guess that means printing.)

Could you send us any information on the history of the Presidential Seal and the symbols that were used?

Can you please send us two copies of things so we will each be able to have a copy including your signature.

A couple of your admirers.

(These kids are in second grade!)

*　　*　　*

Would you like to read an excellent letter from a schoolteacher? This one gets an "A":

Dear Mr. President:

As faculty advisor to the 1969 edition of PIERING, the yearbook of Pier Avenue School, I have been asked to write to you concerning a matter of great importance to the boys and girls of the eighth grade graduating class.

The yearbook staff has decided to dedicate the 1969 PIERING to the memory of the late and great Dwight David Eisenhower. The staff thought that you might like the opportunity to make a statement of dedication.

Mr. President, the boys and girls realize how busy you are, and they will understand perfectly if you are not able to fulfill their request.

The boys and girls are looking forward to their high school years. I know that it is their collective intention to add to the greatness of the United States of America, not to detract from it.

*　　*　　*

Other adults, full of understandable love for their own children, are not so understanding of the grinding pressure of a President's daily schedule:

Mr. President!

I am writing you in regard to surprising my 12-year old son and his 7th grade class.

I would be very grateful and appreciative if you and Vice President Agnew would take the time and trouble to write.

What you write about, I'm sure you know what would be the most interesting to this age group.

P.S. His grandfather was a "Hard headed" Republican but he passed away in December!

*   *   *

All sorts of people, old and young, "lean" on the President, trying to lure a personal letter or a personally autographed picture out of the White House:

Dear President Richard M. Nixon:

I am planning to take a trip to Canada this summer with the Girl Scouts of America. I thought it would be a good idea if I could take a picture of you and your family and a greeting from you to the Girl Guides of Canada.

*   *   *

On Oct. 14th St. Peter's Evening Guild will hold a dessert card party.

Would it be possible for one of your staff to send an autographed photo of you that we could use as a special award? We feel it would add such a hi-light to our event.

*   *   *

I guess you remember my aunt and uncle. They still live in Temple City, California. They told me that they threw a barbecue to help you get started as a member of the House of Representatives. My father was in the "Class of '48" at Whittier College. He said that you were in the class of '42. I, myself, was born in Whittier at Murphy Hospital. We moved out here to San Clemente in 1964. My mother and I were visiting in Whittier just last week. Aunt Hazel wants to take you for a ride in her 1968 Mercedes-Benz!

*   *   *

As we've said, the President's personal secretary is Miss Rose Mary Woods. A letter from a little boy concerning her popped out of the mailbag one day:

Dear President Nixon,

Maybe when I come back to Washington I will see you. I live in Alliance, Ohio, the Carnation City. We are going to have a parade August 18 I wish you could come.

Well, I will see you, Mr. President. My Dad painted Miss Woods' Dad's house in Sebring, Ohio.

*   *   *

(People send everything to the President:)

It came to my attention that Sharon Jones, 12, had written an article in the local newspaper back in January, and no one had sent it to you . . .

(If no one has sent it to the President—send it!)

*   *   *

Dear Mr President,

I have a 10 year old Brother and he drives me crazy, and I think he could do the same For the North Vietnamese. he's a good 1st Base Man In Little League and I think he ~~will be~~ would be good up on the Front Lines

So If You Please try to draft My brother.

~~Susan~~ A Draft Lover

Susan Lionis
2309 Harrison Street
Glenview Illinois 60025

And now let us close this session with two letters from a different Negro school in Chicago. I don't know why Chicago has so many interesting Negro school kids, but they sure do. This bunch of third graders is pure Bill Cosby:

IF I WERE PRESIDENT

If I were President I would let the schoolteachers have $1,000 a week in cash, and I would buy all the school supples. I would give the poor people money, colths, food, and shoes. I would stop the work I was doing and play with my children. I would pay for all my family's weddings.

* * *

If I were President I would help people that can't walk and can't talk and can't hear and can't write. I will help people who can't see. I will help stores. I will help the schools. I will help teachers. I will help children. I will help men. I will help wotn. I will help babys. I will help grow ups. I will help Cup Scouts. I will help dentists. I will help zoos. I will help lions. I will help zoo keeps.

The End!

The Gushers

Many of the letters can only be described as gushers—they take off at a gallop and never look back. Opening one of these letters is like sticking an icepick through a fire hose:

Dear President Nixon:

My age is 15 and would like to say that I am a republican all the way. I hope you do well in the office of the presidency very much. My English teacher would like to say hello very much. Do you think we will have any negotiations in the Viet Nam war very soon. I hope so very much.

I hope your daughter and son-in-law are fine. Tell Mrs. Nixon hello for me to. Do you like the White House, and your office in the capitol very much. Is it fun to fly in the President's jet? I watched the Balls on TV the other night and want to tell you, you looked very distinct, and most distinguished as us kids would call it. You are a great groovy guy from all of us.

* * *

I am 8 years old. I have 3 brothers. I am in second grade. I like to ride my bike. I like my mother and father. I like to take the grabage pails in. I am fine.

How are you? I hope you are fine. How was your trip to Europe? Can you stop all the smoking?

*   *   *

All the gushy letters aren't long. Long or short, they just take off and go!

Dear Mr. President

how was the war in Viet Nam. It is Nice to meet you. Sometimes I see you on TV. Isn't your name Richard Nixon?

*   *   *

(But most of the gushers have staying power:)

My Dear Mr. President,

I have heard of your trip around the world and of your very good progress. I might say a Republican is the friend of the world.

As I myself a republican I helped fight for the repubicans and got a rewarded letter from Barry Goldwater, our state senate.

As for the moon men Aldrin, Armstrong, and Collins, I wish them good luck getting out of the quarentene and no upset stomachs from all the good food which is provided from your family.

I hope you'll give my regards to your wife and kids and good luck through their lives in the Whitehouse even if it is only for 4 years. Maybe you can get the presidency in 1972 and make it another 4 years.

*   *   *

"Do you like your white house? Do you have any bakers at your house? Have you got a bathroom in your house? Do you have any sacks in your house to put your garbage in?"

Dear President Nixon,

Please, just call me Jes. I would like to be a lawyer. But I'm a girl. And I do not know one thing about the law! Could you help me? How did you grow up? All I know is your father was a storekeeper and you became a lawyer. Am I right? Do you like to read books? I do. It gives me answers to my questions. I also like to find out information and for entertament. There are eciting books happy, sad and comedy. Here is my picture. Will you send your picture to me. Giant size of your smiling, please. My sister just had another baby! She has three now. I am an aunt to all three and Godmother to them all. How about that?

*   *   *

Dear President Nixon,

I would like you to know about an amazing coincidence that occurred. Recently, I read an article about the music that was piped in to the west wing executive offices being cut off. The article said that you and your family enjoy listening to a variety of melodies, ranging from classical to pop. It also said that among your favorites are the "Impossible Dream," "Born Free" and the "Zhivago" theme song.

Well, it happens that I play the piano, and those three songs are among the songs I play. I am thirteen years old, and have been playing the piano for three years.

So, in conclusion, I would just like to say that I was very surprised to find that our tastes are so similiar, and I hope that this short letter has proven interesting to you.

*   *   *

I'm a fourth grader at Roosevelt Elementary School. Our class was assigned to write V.I.P. letters to some important person. Next to Bob Hope you are my choice of important persons. I have a few questions to ask you.

1. When and how did you start getting ready to be President?

2. Do you have a hobby?

3. Does it take a lot of money to be a President cause I don't have a lot but I sure would like to be a President or a congressman one day.

4. Could you send me a picture?

Sure hope I can see you some day if you ever get to Oklahoma.

*   *   *

Dear Mr. President,

Happiness is being invited to the White House Religious Service,

Happiness is receiving a Presidential Pen or flag,

Happiness is having a Mother who is Capricorn (Jan. 8) same as the President.

Happiness is having a birthday on June 14 (Flag day—13 years old).

Happiness is having a wonderful Dad and three brothers who help me with math. (two are National Merit Finalists).

and one is a pianist.

*   *   *

I would like to wish you good luck. I hope you will get a chance to stop the war in Vietnam. I hope you will like the White House. It may be hard to be president, but sometimes you can get the hang of it.

*   *   *

Dear Mr. President,

I hope you are enjoying your role as the President of the United States.

I too am a President, But I am not enjoying it what so ever.

My role is the President of the Junior Board of the Villa Espana Condominium.

This "Country", as I call it, is in utter chaos. I have selected My Vice-President Just as you did. "Steve Orbach" is his name and he has all the Qualifications of a Vice-President.

I am 13 years old and I try to Be a good leader, But Nobody listens to me. In the past I have thought of giving up and impeaching myself.

Mr. Nixon in your Opinion what should I do?

Sincerely,

LARRY MARKS

Dear President Nixon.

I wish that I could be President because I would take good care of the U.S. But you would have to help me a little bit beccause I do not no now to do it.

*   *   *

(*Back to the marathon group:*)

I am writing this letter to tell you about my view of the world. First, I'll tell you a little bit about myself. I am going to go into 6th grade in the fall at Indian Trail Jr. High School. I live at home with my father, mother, sister, and dog. My father works at U.S. Steel, my mother works as a secretary, and my sister going into 7th grade, and my dog 8 months old. I play flute in the band.

One thing that bothers me is people, there's too many things wrong with people on this earth. Some people litter, don't vote, don't obey laws, don't respect others, and some are traders.

*   *   *

Dear Nixon.

I love you. Where is Mrs. Nixon? I love her to. do you have to big girl's I love them to. I have 4 sisters they are nice to me do you have a dog?

*   *   *

(*Quite a few of the kids wear their political hearts on their sleeves—ready to go with the winner:*)

At first I was all for Humphry but now that you are President things have changed. Now I'm glad that you are President.

Things have really changed. Your the best. You are the Perfect man.

(I'll say one thing for this boy—when he switches parties, he goes all the way.)

* * *

Mr. the President,

We live in FRANCE in a little town named Nexon—this name is almost like your family name. We are a few girls between 12 years old and 15 years old; we constitute a club: the "Alfa Club." We like the U.S.A. it is a great and beautiful country which attracts us.

We write to you because we think you embody the U.S.A. and the Americans and we want to tell you:

"We admire your country and its inhabitants."

(This letter was signed by a whole bunch of little French girls, whose names were very hard to read.)

* * *

I am a sophmore in the Moundridge High School. I am writing you this letter because I need some help on a report I am going to give at school. The thing that I wanted to ask of you was to send me some pamphlets of all the important and historical buildings and statues in Washington.

Half of our sophmore class was hoping and praying that you would get elected. I tell you one thing if the voting age wouldn't have been 18, and would have been 16, we would have gave you a few more votes.

* * *

"Dear president Nixon,

Yesterday I called the White house and a lady answered and I said would you please take a note for president Nixon so the lady said I'll connect you with Mr. Anderson so I waited a second and Mr. Anderson said hello and I said hello and asked if he would tell president Nixon that I said to have a happy Easter and Mr. Anderson said O.K. and I said thank you and good-by and I've been wondering if you got my note yet and I hope you did."

* * *

Hi! I am so glad that you're the President. I'll bet you and your wife are glad too. I hope when I grow up I will be something special too. My friend and I always play dress up. And we pretend we're movie stars. My cousin Mike plays dress up with me sometimes and he pretends that he's the President and I'm his wife. Well, write back soon.

* * *

These kids' letters are like snowflakes. Just when you think that you've seen every possible variation, the next one will be something brand-new:

Dear Pres. Nixon,

I am in the second grade. My last name is Nixon, too. Do you think we are related?

* * *

Dear Mr. President,

I am 8. I want to be a politician. I want to help Indians, Negrows, and white people in poverty. I want them to have homes that are good, jobs and education for their children and themselves. If I become president I will do this, but I will not be hasty.

(*Sound thinking.*)

*   *   *

Dear Mr. President R.M. Nixon,

I am only 9 years old and are trying to help this country too. I hope I don't make any arors because I'm supposed to be a straight a student.

*   *   *

Dear Presedent Nixon,

Congratulations Mr. President! Would you please tell me what type of work you do.

8

"Has Anybody in Your Family Had Warts?"

Many of the children write to the President on a basis of unbelievable intimacy.

Small boys write to the President as though he were Uncle Charley.

Small girls get crushes on the President. This is understandable, since small girls can get a crush on practically anything— an astronaut, a horse, a cigar store Indian . . . But while understandable, it's still startling to read some of these little-girl letters to the President of the United States.

Dear Mr. Nixon:

I would truly like for you to send me a letter about you and your family and the White House. I would like to read it. I am truly in love with you. Please don't let your wife see this. Well, send me something.

P.S. You're my favorite honey.

*   *   *

(*Or this one:*)

Dear President Nixon,

I love you. I am in the third grade. If you want to write me a letter, I will give you my address.

* * *

(*Many of the little girls are still confused over the difference between "love" and "like":*)

I love you. Becusse you are nice becusse you are write! I like you.

* * *

In addition to the occasional romantic hang-ups, kids write to the President about anything:

I'm twelve years old and have 4 brothers and two more sisters. I think I make fairly good marks in school. (but I don't like my teacher for personal reasons.)

* * *

Boy, is it keen to have a president who isn't square. All the kids in my class say you are a real swinger. I hope you aren't upset. It is a compliment to be called a swinger. It is cool.

Maybe they won't call you a swinger in the history books but to us you will always be the Chief swinger of the U.S.A.

* * *

Dear Presedent Nixon

would you please inform me of the yongest age porsabill for a job. The reason I am writing this is that I am going on ten and would like to em some extra mony to start supporting myself.

*   *   *

You sure did have us worried Wednesday nite when the helicopters had trouble landing in the fog. Now sir you must be very careful and shuld get home a little earlyier. My dad told me you would be in office eight years so please be more careful and get more rest. say hellow to Mrs. Nixon.
P.S. My Dad had to go to porto rico for a week.

*   *   *

Dear Mr. President,

Well, this might sound a little strange, you being a big man and all, and I'm just an ordinary ten-year old girl, and yet I'm really commuting (!) with the President of the United States! How do you do! You know, it seems so exciting! Me, of all people really writing to you! Now let's get down to business. I'm an average american girl who goes to school daily and takes piano lessons. You have a much greater responsibility. I tell you, it takes a great man to run the U.S. It must be very exciting, but I wouldn't want it. You probably have millions of problems. Don't you ever want to quit? I mean, isn't it hard? Well, I guess I'll turn in now.

*   *   *

Dear Presidt Nixon

Is it fun to sit in the White House? Does it scare you when you go to sleep? Did it scare you when you got elected?

* * *

Is it hard to be President? Do you like to be Presdent? What are you doing?

I am doing better in school and geting my work done faster and better.

* * *

(*Some of the spelling is simply amazing:*)

Dear Mr. Preiserdent

We are studing amry. Can you seen me any kind of imformation or migerzins that you have. If you don't have a any of thim. Them seen me some picture.

(*He added a "Thank you"—spelled correctly.*)

* * *

President's Nixuin may I have some pictures of Apoll 13. David righted to Cape Kentud and got some pictures of Asstroandt of Apoll 13. Can you give me some. Thank you.

(*Some of the lousiest spellers are the most polite!*)

P.S. If you can't give me som of Apoll 13, give me some of you. P.SS. If you can't give me some of you give me some of Apoll 12.

* * *

"The day of the voeting my friend's were talking about who was going to be president and I said Nixson and my friend's said he's no good and one of them he's a fish and I said cool it man he's the one my mother and father are going to voet for. And one of my X friend said 'Well take this for likeing him,' POW right in the eye Mr. president."

(Some of the letter writers were staunch supporters when things were tough:)

I am glad you were elected president. As your fellow citizen, I want to wish you a very happy four years. For your campain I think I helped you a little. My girlfriends and I held up signs in frount of cars. One car stopped and nodded and drove off. Many people honked their horns and some made faces at us.

*　　*　　*

How are you doing being a president. We liked your speaches you been saying over T.V. and Radio. In our school we 5th graders would like to see you some day. In school in the morning we say the Stars Spangle Banner or My Country Tis of Thee. I hope you will always be our president for a while.

*　　*　　*

Other than traveling through outer space, there's no area of greater surprise than the mind of a child. There's no way in this world to predict what they're going to say next:

Dear President Nixon,
I would like to know if you could give me a picture of your family that is very inexpensive or free. Please give me free or inexpensive things I can ooh or awh about. I am 10 years old.

*　　*　　*

(Some of the kids employ the President to listen to their lessons:)

I know my numbers.

$$200+200=400$$
$$400+400=800$$
$$800+800=1600$$
$$1600+1600=3200$$

(At that point he stopped. I guess figuring that nobody could need a number bigger than 3200.)

* * *

One reason for some of the kids writing to the President in what you might call an offhand way is that some of them met him before the mantle of history descended about his shoulders. To them he is of course the President, but he is also the man they met several years before at the so-and-so. They know him. Now that he's President, they still know him.

Dear Mr. Nixon,

You're a real nice guy. If you weren't elected President, I don't know what I would do.

I remember once I was at La Gardia Airport. (I live only three or four blocks away.) You were getting on a plane with your wife and there were some photographers there and there wasn't any one else around so I thought, "Wow! this man's alone!" So I went up to you and said, "Hello, Mr. . . . Mr. . . ." and you said "Nixon." "Hello, Mr. Nixon." You said "Hello" and shook my hand.

Do you collect stamps? I do and am sending you some. I hope you can use them.

*   *   *

President Nixon Dear Sir,

Years ago I saw you at a horse show in New York and I shook your hand and you said to me a few words. When I think of it to myself I say, Just think, I shook the hand of President Nixon and it's hard to believe because it's so hard to these days with all those body guards.

I also saw you making a speech in Pailo, Pa.

*   *   *

But possibly the most amazing letters to the President are those that just treat him as an old friend—good old Uncle Dick:

Dear Mr. Nixon,

My family laughs at me because I love cottage cheese and ketchup "Mm". Isn't that good. Will you please write back and tell them that it's good.

*   *   *

If you have any probem in math call 474-6215.

*   *   *

(Anybody who's ever dealt with children will understand the way some of these kids' letters swing back and forth between grown-up and still-baby:)

Dear Mr. Nixon,
Do you like to be a president?
What do you do for a living?

*   *   *

Dear Mr. President,

My name is Linda Jones and I am in seventh grade at Saint Paul's school. I am doing a Science Project on Warts and I would appreciate very much your help by answering the following questions to complete my survey

1. Has any one in your family had warts and if so who?

2. What was the type of treatment used to get rid of warts?

3. Location of warts?

This is the first wart project done at Saint Paul's school and I am trying trying very hard to do my best.

Thank you for your assistance and prompt reply.

Sincerely,
Linda Jones

(And this one. Have a little patience till you get to the kicker:)

Dear President Nixon:

Congratulations on your speech May 14 on Vietnam and the subsequent withdrawal of 25,000 troops from South Vietnam and 25,000 from other foreign bases. I am sure this will unite the people behind your proposals. This is a time when all the people need the security and knowledge of the reasons behind a President's actions.

We stand on the threshold of the greatest technological achievement of not only the U.S. but of the world.

I would like to say that I agree with several congressmen who think a flag of the United Nations should be planted on the moon. I hope you let everyone know that it was everyone's accomplishment and source of pride.

Now can I get to the point of this letter. Did you ever have to wear braces?

*   *   *

Dear Mr. Nixon,

I think they made a good choice. I think you do good in your work. My sister broke her leg skiing. And my other sister is in South Africa. And I have three brothers. All together we have six children. I play marbles. I am sending my picture. I am in my brouny uniform, and another tooth is loose.

*   *   *

How are you? I'm fine. Is there any riits going on. Is there any pliticul talks going on, if there is name one please. I don't have anything spishul to say so I am going to end my letter.

*   *   *

Your niece Lawrene Nixon is my favorite teacher at Brookhaven School (at any school for that matter). She taught me last year in 5th grade and is going to teach me again in 6th.

At Brookhaven School we have team teaching. Which means each grade is a class. For instance, in 5th grade last year we had four 6th grade classes (I think) and four 5th grade classes (I know). This all seems very normal but all of the 5th and 6th grade classes were overcrowded. So, after a few weeks of this the 6th graders moved into the cafetorium. Then they moved to Tuffree Intermediate School. A couple of days later the four 5th grade classes moved into one room (which is pretty easy to do since most of the rooms don't have any walls at Brookhaven School). We were then one class (at the end of the year we had about 136 kids in our class).

Last year we had 4 reading groups, 4 math groups, 1 English, 1 History-Geography (Miss Nixon taught that), 1 Science and 1 Health group. Each subject had one teacher but sometimes another teacher answers the kids questions.

That was last year. I don't know what's going to happen this coming year.

(Would you mind going over that again?)

* * *

Dear Mr. Nixon,:
What is your favorite sport? Mine is eating.

* * *

I have written to you befor. Dose my name sound fermilyer?

* * *

I am a student at Central. I would like for you to send me a picture of you and as many pounds of information as you can afford.

*   *   *

(*Sometimes some of the kids combine on projects, like Gilbert and Sullivan. This one's from two little girls:*)

Mr. President:

During summer vacation we made up a song tribute to Apollo 11.

Some suggested we send it to the local newspapers. Others, send it to the astronot's wives. But the best suggestion was to send a copy to you. Thanks to my sister.

The tune is to Jingle Bells.

SOARING APOLLO

Soaring on through space,
With triple engine speed.
Three Amercian men,
Fill their countries need.
Apollo's on the moon,
Russia's way behind.
Apollo hurry up
Before they say "It's mine!"
Apollo hurry back,
And bring some samples too,
And when you come back . . .
All people will praise *You!*

*   *   *

"When the astronauts get back ask them if they caught the cow thats been jumping over the moon all these years."

(It's difficult to put some of these letters into any category. You just have to let 'em fly:)

In school we made a bulletin board for Easter we made eggs and wrote our names on them to tell who it was from.

Well I better go now I only have 15 more minutes.

* * *

I hope you enjoyed your trip to Europe. I guess you had so many responsibilities you didn't have much time for sightseeing.

* * *

Dear Richard Nixon

On our Easter trip we had lots of fun. We brout our cat named Bushka.

The first night we camped at the place where the Hollywood filmed "Water hole number three."

The next night we camped at a windy place in deth valley monument. We brout a tent and as we were going to put the stakes in so it wouldent blow away a big wend came along and our tent blew away. But fliny we brout it back. The next night we ate mash Potatoes and beefstoo. The fourth night we camped at a place where we heard some olws. We went home in the rain the last night.

* * *

I will be 8 years old on Nov. 3rd. Thank you, Mr. President.

* * *

Enclosed is a picture of a mural which we made and hung in the corridor. We also took a picture of our bulletin board which was even better, but it didn't turn out.

*   *   *

Dear Mr. Nixon
I helped my mother to put the leters in the envelopes & put the stamps on. & folded the papers.
So why didn't you invite me to the Ball.

*   *   *

It would be nice if I could have your autograph. If you can't give it to me than I would accept your wife and daughters. If they can't I would like your secretarys.

*   *   *

Dear Mr. President,
I saw you at Kennedy Space Center on T.V. last Friday. Did it hurt your eyes when you looked at the blast off? Did you ever get lost in your big house? I get lost in my basement sometimes.

*   *   *

(*Other letters to the President can only be called snitching:*)

My teacher said that you ar a real man because you lost many time but kept on fighting till you won. I am in fifth grade but I like school very much. I think that you should go to school and not play hooky. I know two girl in my room that play hooky and don't go to school. One day they brought a back of Marbarro to school.

*   *   *

(*And one more:*)

Dear President Nixon,

I am six years old, and I'm in the first grade.

Whin is your birthday and do we get that day off like we do George Woshingtons and Abe Lincoln.

9

Every Sparrow
That Falls

The President naturally can't be expected to take care of every sparrow that falls, but many of them fall past his office window. Most of his mail from kids is fortunately happy, since kids are usually happy. But some of the letters are like a cry in the night. Children can be rock-hard honest about sorrow.

Dear President Nixon,

I always watch when you are on television. I am in 4th grade. In the classroom we had a vote on who would win the election. You won!! I was one of the children Who voted for you. I hope if you run for President you will win again.

Tomorrow we are going to be at a wake for my Grandmother Bush. She is my mothers mother. She was the nicest Grandmother any little boy ever had. If you get the time will you say a prayer for her at church next Sunday? She will be buried on Monday at the Chapel Hills Cemetery and it is a very beautiful place at least.

(Did you ever hear human grief expressed any better than that?)

*   *   *

I am afraid to go to school. Could you get me a pass to become teacher and have my teacher become a pupil.

*   *   *

I hope I don't have to go to war but you can Bet I will if I have to. I get haircuts and take baths.

*   *   *

I lickd your speech to win the war. I hope you get my Unkle back home he is mising from my Basball team. I am 7 years old and ned his hlp to win.

*   *   *

My Dear Mr. President:

Last Friday night was graduation night at Pioneer Valley and my brother was one of the graduates. He is the second child in our family to graduate from Pioneer; my brother Freddie graduated in 1967 and then joined the Army and was killed in Vietnam in 1968. My brother Larry who graduated last Friday night plans to join the service in the fall, but he has not as yet made up his mind exactly which branch he will choose.

*   *   *

Some of the kids—many of them—are deeply religious. They start off funny, but then things change:

I am a ninthgrade student and I'm fourteen years old. My limited knowledge of the complicated mechanics required to run and understand good government has brought me to the point where I must speak out and express myself.

I have been told that in the early Bibical days, God granted leaders certain requests providing they prayed a minute each and everyday. Sir, I would pray with you if I knew when you were going to pray, so we could both pray for world peace. God said he would hear every prayer wherever two would gather in his name.

* * *

Dear President Nixon

I hope you have the extra time to read my letter. I am writing to let you know the good things and the bad things. A president is something like a father you can go to the president to listen to your problems as well as your father.

The teen-agers that are in the streets today it is just out rageous. There are so many bad things I can't describe them all. You know what they are. "Please!" try to help us.

* * *

I am writing to tell you about Detroit. I live in the slums of Detroit. I often walk down the street and just stare at the sidewalks. It hurts me just to look at all of the filth and garbage. I have 2 sisters and 1 brother. I don't want the smallest one growing up in a neighborhood like this. I love to go to Bell Isle and watch the fountain at night. It changes colors. I only get to go sometimes. You know how it is. If you understand.

* * *

Wakefield, Va.
March 18, 1969

Dear Mr. President,

I am not an assassinator.
I am just a harmless little
six grade kid. If you have any
spare time I wouldn't mind
having a letter from you just
to show off at school.
Thank you.

Yours truely,
William. R. Stephenson.

Why is it that there is hardly any street lights on certain
streets. This is were all of the burglers come in. Please try
harder to stop crime.

* * *

I would like to tell you something. On Trumbull and Bagley we have a baseball field. And the boys play their regular. And you should see it, cans, glass, bricks, and the bricks are up so high you can't eve play baseball. And it seems horrible because we can't go to the games so we play were it's messy.

*　　*　　*

Old houses need to be torn down. We need new hospital. The rent for the Ralph J. Bunche is too high. The poor people need to be help . . .

*　　*　　*

(How would you like to be President? But in the next letter comes a ray of hope:)

Dear President Nixon,

Why can't these run down neighborhoods get a block committ to gether and organize a big "Clean Up Drive." We had one for our school and when we finished it looked simply beautiful.

10

"Mr. Prezedent, Here's How to Handel It"

Kids, being kids, don't at all mind telling the President how to run the country. Also, being kids, they get right to the point. Here's a letter in its entirety:

Dear Mr. President,

I have been thinking about Viet Nam. Wowdn't it be cheaper to buy it?

*　　*　　*

I wish that you would put something in the space suit for when the space men go out on the moon. Make something so the astronauts do not have to go to the bathroom in the suit.

*　　*　　*

(And a helpful thought from a young economist:)

I am an 8th. grade student, and am interested in the space program, but Mr. Nixon I think it's a waste of our countrys money to look for life on the planets. If there were life up there they would have borrowed money from the United States by now.

*　　*　　*

"Many many years before the white man came, the Indians were living on this land. When the white man came, he took the land which rightly belonged to the Indians."

Dear Sir:

I am ten years old, and I hate what teenagers are doing. I think I know what to do. I watch the "Beverly Hillbillys." Granny loads her shotgun with bacon rine and Rock Salt. She shoots them usualy in the Rearend. Why don't you do this.

* * *

(To a child, little things like plane highjackings are no problem:)

In regard to the plane hi-jackings. Wouldn't it be safer and cheaper to have a weekly shuttle to Cuba from New York or Miami?

* * *

Some of the letters, particularly those from minority groups, are quite severe with the President:

Dear Mr. President,

You have been in the white house long enough, you should stop the war. To many of our black brothers are being kill in the war.

I hope you stop the war before I get there.

If I die in the army it will mass up my whole life.

I was planning on being a basketball player.

* * *

Next time you have a moon walk, Mars walk or other event important enough to declare a national holiday, please see to it that it is not on a national holiday. I need all the vacation I can get.

*   *   *

I am 11 years of age and I have decided to start expressing my views on world affairs.

I enjoy reading the paper and watching the Brinkley news. Sometimes I am shocked at some of the things I read about and see. I think sir, that you should go on T.V. and talk to the parents of the children that are doing the rioting in many of the countrie's schools. Ask these people to take a look at their kids and see if it's worth it to send these kids to school. I am sure that if these kids were working their way through school they would not be rioting.

*   *   *

At 10 or 11 children get very tough; they get an affinity with Marine drill sergeants.

But younger than that some of the kids' solutions to wars are unforgettably delightful:

I am eight years old and in the second garde. If there mad at each other why should there be a war, Why don't they just don't talk to each other and not be there friends?

*   *   *

Some of the slightly older kids, of course, sound tough because they haven't any idea what they're talking about:

Dear Mr. President,

I have a 10-year old Brother and he drives me crazy. And I think he could do the same for the North Vietnamese. So if you Please try to draft My brother.

(Now she doesn't really mean that!)

* * *

My friends and I are writing this because we want to find out a answer to a question. The question is, does David Eisenhower have to go to service? If he doesn't have to go, why not?
P.S. If you have the time we all would appreciate a answer. We will pass it on to the other kids in town.

(Dear Kids: Up to now, David Eisenhower has had the same military exemptions countless other young men have had—he has been a college student maintaining satisfactory grades, and in addition he is married. Now that he has graduated from college, he is fulfilling his obligation to his country in the Navy. His father-in-law, Mr. Richard Nixon of Washington, D.C., also served in the Navy.)

* * *

3/5/69
19 Glacier Drive
Smith town N.Y.
(11787)

Dear President, NIXON,

I just finesed My
homework A thought of a way
to stop the war, By
drafting women because
who would shot at a women.
I think it might work
do you? I Have Had enough
of this terrible war
didn't you?

Sincerly,
Bruce Sonschen

I would like to know why you drafted my mother's boyfriend. My mother is very mad about it. I would like your personnel reply.

*   *   *

Dear Sir

On the date of Apollo 11's splash down, while you were on the recovery ship USS Hornet, the TV viewer got a look at your personnel marine helicopter. I would like to inquire why the flag on your helicopter was on backwards, when the letters were frontwards.

*   *   *

I wish the color of the flag was pink yellow, green, purple and white. It would be groovey if you would let us teens get a wife.

*   *   *

(*The following was printed at the end of quite a long letter. It was what you might call a summing up:*)

WHAT ARE YOU, THE PRESIDENT GOING TO DO ABOUT THE BARE NECESSITIES OF LIFE?

*   *   *

(*Among all the stop-the-war letters was this one—which is a little puzzling:*)

In this letter I want to say something about the war going on. We love the Japanese for what they are, but we are killing them for what they think and we think.

(You're a couple of wars behind. Have you been up in the attic reading old newspapers? You're going to have to catch up. There's nothing less interesting than an old war.

(Try to get hold of one of today's newspapers. You'll be amazed at what's going on. The Japanese are now our friends. Really.)

*   *   *

(One little kid had a quick solution to the Vietnam situation:)

We can just chicken out and run. Let them think we are chickens. It may save many lives.

*   *   *

But of course the kids want the President to do a lot of things other than stop the war. There's another letter-writing phalanx, also no doubt prodded to the mailbox by teachers and/or parents, who want him to stop all this space nonsense and spend the money in good works here on earth. Some of these anti-moon letters get pretty sharp.

Dear President Nixon

I heard you talk to the men on the moon Sunday night. I would like to know how much that long distance phone call did cost? I would like to compare the cost of calling my brother in the Marines stationed in California. Thank you.

*   *   *

"My Mommy and Daddy says our country spends too much money. Will we end up poor Like Rome did when they fell down?"

But there are always the other letters, from the other side:

Dear President Nixon;

I am a young man in the seventh grade.

On Sunday, I heard since NASA didn't have anything planned to do after the "moon mission," that their budget may get cut *again!*;, or the military may get it, or NASA might be done away with totally!;, by order of the President of the United States of America! That is YOU!

You can prevent it from occurring and, if I were you, I wouldn't just cut off NASA because it is too big a project, too much money, time and effort and too many people are involved to just shut it down, furthermore space travel is very popular among the people.

I, and some of my friends think space exploration is important because we could use the moon for a place to spread the exploding populus, to erect "hot houses" to help feed the world, and as a point of strategic and tactical bases.

*   *   *

By far the bulk of the kids' letters about Vietnam consist of Stop the war . . . cut and run . . . come home. But some of the kids are fire-breathing hawks:

I don't believe that we are fighting the Viet Nam war in the right way. We are not getting anywhere by just fooling around. We should bomb the major areas of North Viet Nam until they are of no real use to the Viet Cong. We should keep the Viet Cong out of the South for good and invade the North ourselfs. This is the way a war should be fought.

*   *   *

There is one thing wrong if we stop the war. They'll move in on us. Eventually they'll keep moving in on us. Pretty soon they'll own all our land and we will be ruled by them.

*   *   *

This war should never have been a problem in the first place. If we had gone into Vietnam like the Russians went into Czechoslavakia, we would never be in the position we are in now.

We beat Germany and Japan combined in only five years! We should bomb important areas such as Haiphong Harbor, warehouses, and war factories in North Vietnam. Close up the Hoe Chi Minh trail for good. Get the North Vietcong out of South Vietnam. Wreck more bridges and railroads and convoys . . .

(You kids should have known a fellow named General Sherman, who once took a trip through Georgia. You kids and Sherman would have got along great.)

*   *   *

Mr. President,

We have talked about the Pueblo and its capture. We know that all the secret papers were hard to burn. Our class has heard about a new kind of paper that dissolves quickly in water. Have you heard about it? We tried it out and it worked! We are sending a sample for you to see and the address of the company that makes it.

*   *   *

(And if you think inflation hits only adults:)

Dear Mr. President Nixon:

It's not fair, that we have to pay tax to the ice cream man. Lost year I paid 20¢ for my favorite chocolate ice cream bar. Now I pay 25¢ plue tax. My allowance is only 50¢ a week. I could have tow ice cream bars now I can only buy one. Mr. President, I would like to know what you do with my tax money.

*   *   *

(From the Atlantic to the Pacific, from kids everywhere, complaints, complaints, complaints. Lately nobody likes anything:)

Presi. Nixon

I am writing you concerning my dislike to riding school buses. I am up *tight* from the time my mother pull me out of bed ealry in the morning untill I return home at night. I can't eat breakfast *"relaxed"* just gulp down a fiew bites while my mother keep up that "hurry hurry or you will miss your bus." I get on a bus that is now full of kids. The flu bug is flying all over the bus. I breathe all of these germs plus the engin exaust, and in two weeks I am sick nad out of shcool.

Now mr president, I ask you: wouldn't all of this tax money that is spent on buses year after year with no ent in sight be better used to build more nice buildings for schools where the kids could enjoy a nice morning walk to and from school. This would build up mussels also apitites, and minds.

*   *   *

In Social Studies we were talking about other countries. We think that South Americans, Canadians, and other people on the American Continents don't like us being called the Americans, because they are Americans too. Our class voted on some names and we decided on the United Statesmen.

(Now just a darn minute. That would make the actual name of our country, "The United States of the United Statesmen." How do you think that would look?)

* * *

In regard to the uniforms you have given to the Washington White House police, I would like to say they are extremely ugly.

I would also like to say the police are instituted to protect the people, not strut like roosters. Also fat, middle-aged policemen only look good, to me, in blue.

* * *

My dream is to be a police officer. I am eight years old. Please let me be a police Please.

* * *

Another mass interest of the children today is, as they say, "pulution."

"I think you can stop the war. If you do you will probaly go down in history like Rodolf the Red Nose Reindeer."

Mr. Nixon,

I have an idea for pulution, put it in sacks and boxes then put it in an airplane, and drop off the pulution into a active volcano. When it acts up we will have more land. (!)

* * *

On pollution, children get right to the point just as on anything else:

Dear Presedent Nixon,

I think pollution is a disgrace. Tell people how it kills animals, how it dirties the water. Tell them pretty soon they will have to wear gas masks.

Even my mother is polluting rivers. She uses deterents.

* * *

Dear Mr. President,

I hope you can help us we Just found out that a little bird got killed by pollution the bird was eating some trash and it got sick.

* * *

You know—today's kids may stop pollution. They feel something about it.

* * *

And on the international scene, these kids see things pretty clearly:

Dear President R. Nixon,

How are you doing? We have been talking about Vietnam. I think you should bring our men home. Russia is a little smater than us. They just send money and guns, no men, but we send money, guns and men.

Bring the men home and just send guns and money.

I didn't vote for you, but I'll try to be happy with you.

*   *   *

Dear President Nixon,

I am a 5th grader. I am sure you will find a solution to the Viet Nam situation. Isn't it funny we always get stuck with the wars.

*   *   *

(*Some of the kids take up quite a few suggestions in one letter:*)

I saw your Inauguration on TV. I saw the guards to protect you from rocks and sticks flying through the air. Now I think that these people that did this are reel bum sports and here is what I think you should do about the war. First do not try to drop any bombs on towns you will kill many civilains, children, babys. Second do not shoot any civilians. Third try to have peace talks with Korea, North Vietnam or any other country that we are against. Do not give equipment to the Mozlans or Isralitites that is the way R.F.K. got shot which as you no was very sad. Forth try to not let people with wild animals in the seaports because as you remember a little boy in Miami Florida got mald by a cheeta.

*   *   *

Your political life and mine are almost parralell. I lost my bid for the Presidency in 6th grade. I lost by a closer margin in a bid for a lesser position, and now I plan to make a big comeback.

*   *   *

I saw you call the moon on T.V. Sunday night. I called the operator and asked to call the moon. She said When you get the number I will get you through. Is it an unlisted number?

*   *   *

Mr. President,

I'm a girl fifteen years old.

I sincerely want to become a Congressional page but have been barred because of my sex. The Congressmen tell me about tradition and the Sargeant at Arms of the Senate says "The physical facilities in the Senate chambers and cloakrooms do not lend themselves to the adjustment which, in my opinion, would be necessary."

If that statement is true, then an appalling state of discrimination exists not only against prospective page, but women legislators as well.

It's kind of ironic that Congress which passes bills against discrimination should be practicing it. By not giving me or any other girl a chance, their contradicting themselves.

I hope you can give me some advice so that I may help to correct this injustice.

(The problems a President has! And these are only his kid problems!)

*   *   *

Please President Nixon on your recess maybe you could answer my question. Here is my question. If you were 10 years old how would you help your country?

*   *   *

And now, much as we hate to, it comes time to end this book. We wish we could put in all the letters that the kids have written to the President. They were all wonderful. But to include them all would have taken a book fourteen feet thick.

What shall we pick as our final letter? . . . The most profound? . . . The most hilarious? . . .

No, let's finish with this one:

Mr. President,

Howdy. How are you, good I'm fine too. Gotta go. Bye now.